PEARSON LON

PEARSON English Learning System

Workbook

Anna Uhl Chamot

Jim Cummins

Sharroky Hollie

PEARSON

Upper Saddle River, New Jersey • Boston, Massachusetts • Chandler, Arizona • Glenview, Illinois

Pearson Longman Cornerstone 1A, 1B
Workbook

PEARSON English Learning System

Staff credits: The people who made up the Cornerstone team, representing editorial, production, design, manufacturing, and marketing, are John Ade, Rhea Banker, Daniel Comstock, David Dickey, Gina DiLillo, Johnnie Farmer, Nancy Flaggman, Charles Green, Karen Kawaguchi, Ed Lamprich, Niki Lee, Jaime Leiber, Chris Leonowicz, Tara Maceyak, Linda Moser, Laurie Neaman, Leslie Patterson, Sherri Pemberton, Diane Pinkley, Liza Pleva, Susan Saslow, Chris Siley, Loretta Steeves, Kim Steiner, and Lauren Weidenman.

Text composition: The Quarasan Group, Inc.

Illustrations: Kathryn Mitter 4 top right, 5, 6 top right; **Kathryn Adams, Megan Montague Cash, Chris Reed, Michael Sloan** 6 middle left, 6 middle center, 6 middle right, 6 bottom left, 6 bottom center, 10 bottom right, 25, 26, 30 left bottom, 36 left middle, 42 left top middle, 50 top left, 51, 52 right, 52 left, 53 top right, 56 top left, 60, 62 bottom middle left, 66, 68 left bottom middle, 76 middle, 80, 92, 94 middle, 94 bottom, 96 top middle,103 middle, right, 108 top left, 108 bottom left, 134 top left, 134 bottom left, 146 top middle left, 146 bottom left; **Don Tate** 10 top right, 11, 12, 21; **Kathy Wilburn** 12 bottom; **Mary Roja** 16 top, 17, 147; **Apryl Stott** 30, 31, 32 right, **Sue Miller** 26 left, 32 left, 37, 42 top, 43, 44; **Barbara Spurll** 32, 36; **Drew-Brook Cormack** 94 top right, 98; **Mark Stephens** 72 top right, 108 top right,109, 110, 125; **Anne Kennedy** 134 top right, 135, 136; **Melanie Siegel** 108; **Linda Pierce** 146 top right

Photos: Unit 3: 56 top right, Markus Gebauer/Shutterstock; 57 middle, Owen Franken/Corbis; 57 bottom, L. Dantas/Abril/Zefa/Corbis; 62 top right, PhotoEdit Inc.; 63 top, Stock Connection; 63 bottom, PhotoEdit Inc; 64 left, Corbis NY; 64 right, iophoto/Shutterstock; 68 top, Altrendo Images/Getty Images; 69, Sven Creutzman/Corbis; 70 Photo Researchers Unit 4: 82 top, Barrie Watts/DK Images; 83-84, Barrie Watts/DK Images; 88, Photolibrary Pty. Ltd./Index Open; 89 Cathy Melloan Unit 5: 114 top, Randy Faris/Corbis; 115, Randy Faris/Corbis; 120 top, Bettmann/Corbis; 121, Bill Manns/Corbis; 122, The Granger Collection, NY; 126, Bettmann/CORBIS; 130 The Granger Collection, NY Unit 6: 140, Peter Greste/Reuters/Corbis; 141, AP Wide World Photos; 142 left, Dorling Kindersley; 142 right, National Geographic

ISBN-13: 978-1-4284-3484-4
ISBN-10: 1-4284-3484-4

Printed in the United States of America
5 6 7 8 9 10 V0N4 16 15 14 13

CONTENTS

UNIT 1

UNIT 2

UNIT 3

CONTENTS

Name _____ Date _____

Vocabulary

A. Fill in the missing letters to complete the word.

1. new   ____ e ____

2. like   ____ i ____ e

3. my   m ____

4. backpack   ____ a c k ____ a c k

5. you   y o ____

Sight Words
like
my
you

Story Words
new
backpack

B. Write the word that completes each sentence.

6. I like _____ hat.

7. My hat is _____ .

8. Do _____ like it?

9. I have a red _____ .

10. I _____ my red backpack.

3

Phonics

A. Draw a line to the letter that stands for the sound at the *beginning* of the word.

1.   s

2.   m

3.   a

4.    d

B. Circle the words with the short *a* sound.

5. Sam had a backpack.

6. I am Sam.

Name _____ Date _____

Think It Over

Reread to tell about the story.

I am sad.

I am new.

I am Sam.

A. Circle the letter of the word that correctly completes the sentence. Then write the word.

1. Sam is new so she is _____ .

   a. big   **c.** sad

   b. old   **d.** happy

2. Sam meets a kid named _____ .

   a. Sam   **c.** May

   b. Jin   **d.** Jen

3. Sam has a new _____ .

   a. hat   **c.** bed

   b. pal   **d.** dog

B. Look at the pictures. Fill in the chart with words that name things in a school. Draw your school.

bike   book   crayons

desk   house   map   pencil

Name _____ Date _____

Grammar

Use **I am** to talk about you.

Use **not** to talk about things that are not true.

Use **are you** to ask a question.

Choose a word from the box. Complete the sentence.

am   are

Example: I <u>am</u> six.

1. I _____ not six.

2. _____ you happy?

3. Yes, I _____ .

4. I _____ new.

5. _____ you new at school?

Writing

Choose the correct word. Write the sentence with the correct word.

Example: I (am, are) _____ new.

I am new.

1. _____ you happy? (Am, Are)

_____

- - - - - - - - - - - - - - - - - - -

_____

2. Yes, I _____ happy. (is, am)

_____

- - - - - - - - - - - - - - - - - - -

_____

3. I _____ Paco. (are, am)

_____

- - - - - - - - - - - - - - - - - - -

_____

4. _____ you Ana? (Am, Are)

_____

- - - - - - - - - - - - - - - - - - -

_____

5. I _____ not Ana. (am, are)

_____

- - - - - - - - - - - - - - - - - - -

_____

Name _____ Date _____

Vocabulary

A. Write the word that completes each sentence.

Sight Words

see

is

little

1. I can _____ with my eyes.

2. A baby is _____ .

3. A _____ has pretty wings.

4. Mel _____ happy.

Story Words

butterfly

frog

B. Write the letters in the right order to make a word.

5. e s e   _____

6. g f r o   _____

7. s i   _____

8. e t l y f b t u r   _____

9. t l i t e l   _____

Phonics

Circle the letter that stands for the sound at the *beginning* of the word.

1.   e   a   m

2.  m   l   d

3.   f   h   t

4.  m   a   e

5.   l   t   e

6.  f   l   d

7.   s   l   t

Name _____ Date _____

Think It Over

Reread to tell about the story.

See Ted.

Ted is a fat tadpole.

He is a fat, fat tadpole.

Ted is big.

He sits and sits.

Ted is a frog.

A. Answer the questions.

1. What is Ted like when he is new?

   He is _____ .

2. When does Ted get big?

   He gets big after he _____ .

3. What is Ted now?

   Ted is a _____ .

B. **Look at the pictures below. Think about how a tadpole becomes a frog. Write *1, 2, 3,* and *4* to show the right order.**

_____

_____

_____

_____

Name _____ Date _____

Grammar

> Use **he** for a boy, **she** for a girl, and **it** for a thing.
>
> Use the verb **is** with *he, she,* and *it.*
>
> Use **is** before *he, she,* and *it* to ask a question.

Circle the correct word for the sentence.

Example: Is Bill nice?

Yes, (he̲) (he, she) is nice.

1. Is Ana funny?

   Yes, (he, she) is funny.

2. (Is, Are) Ms. Bell a teacher?

   Yes, (she, he) is.

3. (Is, Are) Ted six?

   Yes, (she, he) is six.

4. (Is, Are) the bag new?

   No, (it, he) is not.

Writing

Read the sentences. Find the error in each one. Write the correct sentence.

Example: Is Mr. Hart a teacher? Yes, <u>she</u> is.

Yes, <u>he is</u>.

1. Is Ted six? No, she is not.

No,

2. Is the bag new? No, she is not.

No,

3. Is Ms. Cho sad? Yes, he is.

Yes,

4. Is the pencil new? Yes, he is.

Yes,

Name _____ Date _____

Vocabulary

A. Write the word that completes each sentence.

1. My shoes are _____ big!

2. He has _____ cups.

3. Please help _____ .

4. This game is _____ .

5. I _____ a cat.

Sight Words
have
me
too

Story Words
three
fun

B. Circle the vocabulary words in the Word Search.

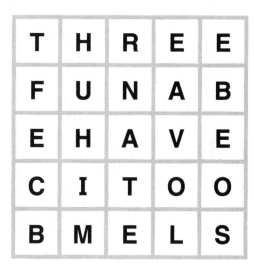

T	H	R	E	E
F	U	N	A	B
E	H	A	V	E
C	I	T	O	O
B	M	E	L	S

Phonics

A. Circle the word with the short *i* sound.

1. We can sit.

2. Jen did that.

3. Ed bit the apple.

4. Pat has a pet pig.

B. Circle the letter that stands for the sound at the *beginning* of the word.

5.   p   m   d

6.    p   n   e

7.   l   f   p

8.   a   n   s

Name _____ Date _____

Think It Over

Reread to tell about the story.

I am Tip.

I am sad.

Kim is sad, too.

Kim is a pal.

A. Answer the questions.

1. Who tells the story?

_____ tells the story.

2. How are Tip and Kim the same?

They are both _____ .

3. How are Tip and Kim different?

Kim is a person and Tip is a _____ .

B. Fill in the T-chart. Tell how the city and the country are alike and different.

City and Country	
alike	**different**
_____	_____
_____	_____
_____	_____
_____	_____
_____	_____

Name _____ Date _____

Grammar

Use **we** for you and other people.

Use **they** for two or more people, places, or things.

Use **are** with *we* and *they*.

Circle the correct word. Write the word.

Example: (Is, (Are)) the pals nice?

Yes, they <u>are</u>.

1. (Is, Are) the pencil new?

Yes, it _____.

2. (Is, Are) the pals fun?

Yes, they _____.

3. (Is, Are) he six?

No, he _____ not.

4. (Is, Are) they students?

Yes, they _____.

Writing

Choose the correct word. Write the sentence with the correct word.

Example: We (is, are) in class.
We are in class.

1. We _____(is, are)_____ students.

_____

- -

_____

2. She _____(is, are)_____ my teacher.

_____

- -

_____

3. You _____(is, are)_____ at school.

_____

- -

_____

4. _____(Is, are)_____ they new pencils?

_____

- -

_____

Name _____ Date _____

Review

**Answer the questions after reading Unit 1.
You can go back and reread to help find the
answers.**

1. Circle all the words with the short *a* sound.

   I am sad.

2. Who does Sam meet at school?

   She meets _____ .

3. In *I Met Ted*, what do you read about first? Circle
   the letter of the right answer.

   a. Ted is a frog.

   b. A caterpillar meets Ted the tadpole.

   c. Ted is a fat, fat tadpole.

   d. The caterpillar is in a home.

4. What is the caterpillar by the end of *I Met Ted*?

   _____

   _____

5. Circle all the words with the short *e* sound.

Ted is little. Ted met a pal.

6. In *Tip,* how is Kim like Ann, Ed, and Mel? Circle the letter of the right answer.

   a. She has a van like them.

   b. She is sad like them.

   c. She is Tip's pal like them.

   d. She has the same home as them.

7. Circle all the words with the short *i* sound.

Kim is Tip's pal. Tip sits in a van.

8. What were three animals in the stories you read? Write a sentence about each animal.

Name _____ Date _____

Writing Workshop: Write a Paragraph

You will write a paragraph. Look at Beth's paragraph.

I am Beth. My pal is Gina. She is nice. My pal is Joe. We like the playground.

I. Prewrite List your friends. Tell something about each person.

Person	Something about him or her

2. **Draft** Write a paragraph. Use the ideas from your list.

I am _____.

_____

- -

_____

- -

_____

- -

_____

- -

_____

- -

3 & 4. **Revise and Edit** Look for errors in your paragraph. Correct the errors to make your writing better. Go to page 56 of the Student Book and use the Editing Checklist.

5. **Publish** Make a clean copy of your paragraph on another sheet of paper. Share it with the class.

Name _____ Date _____

Fluency

A. Listen to the words in each row. Which word sounds different? Circle it. Read each row of words aloud.

1. am   are   have   sad

2. bed   egg   red   she

3. big   fish   five   ink

B. Listen. Then write the words with the same sounds in the correct boxes.

cat   desk   ink   map   pet   pig

      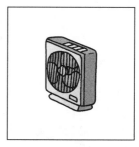

Fluency

C. **Take turns reading the sentences aloud with a partner. Use your finger to follow the words.**

> I have a new dog.

> Ed has a little fish.

> The elephant is big.

D. **Read the sentences in Part C again. Draw a line from each sentence to the correct picture.**

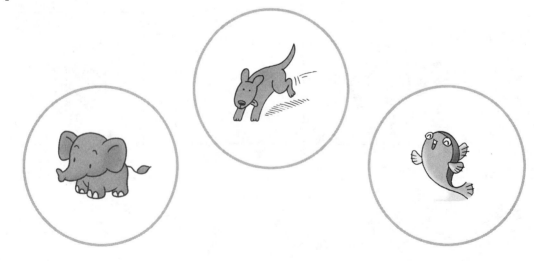

Name _____ Date _____

Learning Checklist

Phonics

- ☐ Short *a*: *d, m, s*
- ☐ Short *e*: *f, l, t*
- ☐ Short *i*: *n, p*

Strategies

- ☐ Preview
- ☐ Sequence
- ☐ Compare and Contrast

Grammar

- ☐ *Be* Verbs
- ☐ Pronouns: *He, She, It*
- ☐ Pronouns: *We, They*

Writing

- ☐ Draw a picture of your face. Write about you.
- ☐ Draw a picture of a classmate. Write about your classmate.
- ☐ Draw a picture of your class. Write about your class.
- ☐ Writing Workshop: Write a Paragraph

Listening and Speaking

- ☐ Describe a Good Friend

Name _____ Date _____

Vocabulary

A. Write the word that completes each sentence.

Sight Words

he

she

about

1. Is _____ your dad?

2. Lots of _____ came to the play.

3. Jen mailed a _____ .

4. I am happy _____ my new backpack.

Story Words

people

letter

5. Is _____ your mom?

B. Write the letters in the right order to make a word.

6. p l e p e o   _____

7. o u t a b   _____

8. e s h   _____

9. l e t r e t   _____

10. e h   _____

Phonics

A. Circle the word with the short *o* sound.

1. net   nut   not

2. log   leg   lag

3. red   rod   rid

4. on   an   in

B. Write the letter that stands for the sound at the *beginning* of the word.

5. _____

6. _____

7. _____

8. _____

Name _____ Date _____

Think It Over

Reread to tell about the story.

Dot can help Ned send a letter.

Sal can help Mom and Tam.

She can take Mom and Tam on the bus.

A. Answer the questions.

1. What is Dot's job? Dot is a _____ .

2. What is Sal's job? Sal is a _____ .

3. Who can Sal help? Sal can help

   _____ .

4. Who are Dot and Sal? Dot is a _____

   and Sal is a _____ .

Unit 2

B. Read the sentences in each column. Add words about the story.

K – What I Know	W – What I Want to Know	L – What I Learned
I know that _____ can help Ned.	I want to know how Dot can help _____ .	I learned that Dot can Ned send a _____ .
I know that _____ can help Mom and Tam.	I want to know how Sal can help _____ and _____ .	I learned that Sal can take Mom and Tam on the _____ .

Name _____   Date _____

Grammar

Use **can** + **verb** to talk about things people are able to do.

Use **can** + **not** + **verb** to talk about things people are not able to do.

Use **can** + **subject** + **verb** to ask a question.
cannot = **can't**

Complete the sentences. Use *can, cannot, or can't*.

Example: <u>can</u> you ski? Yes, <u>I can</u>.

1. _____ he swim?

   No, he _____ .

2. _____ she play soccer?

   Yes, she _____ .

3. _____ he sing?

   Yes, he _____ .

4. _____ she run?

   No, she _____ .

Writing

Read the sentences. Add a period to each sentence. Write the sentences.

Example: I am six I can swim

<u>I am six. I can swim</u>.

1. Jim can sing They can sing

_____

- -

2. They can skate They cannot swim

_____

- -

3. You can play soccer I can't play

_____

- -

4. They can ski You can ski

_____

- -

5. Avi and Dan can run They can play

_____

- -

Name _____ Date _____

Vocabulary

A. **Write the word that completes each sentence.**

I. That pie was sweet and

_____ .

2. I have _____ job to do
after this one.

3. We _____ at a
picture book.

4. An apple is a good _____ .

5. I pick _____ cap I want to put on.

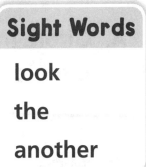

Sight Words

look

the

another

Story Words

delicious

snack

B. **Circle four vocabulary words in the Word Search.**

T	H	E	C	X	O	U	S	B
R	K	A	N	O	T	H	E	R
D	E	L	I	C	I	O	U	S
I	Y	J	D	V	L	O	O	K

35

Phonics

A. Circle the word that tells about the picture. Say the word.

1.	rug	pad	bug
2.	cup	bus	dog
3.	at	up	cub
4.	cat	bud	bed

B. Write the letter that stands for the sound at the *beginning* of the word.

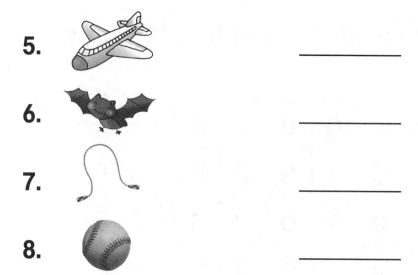

5. _____

6. _____

7. _____

8. _____

Name _____ Date _____

Think It Over

Reread to tell about the story.

Bud and his dad can hop to the shop.

Bud can have milk and jam.

A. Answer the questions.

1. Who is in the story?

_____

- -

_____

2. What is the story about?

_____

- -

_____

3. How does Bud get to the shop?

_____

- -

_____

4. What does Bud drink?

_____

- -

B. Reread the story. Then complete the chart with words from the box.

| shops | milk | ice cream | ham | jam |

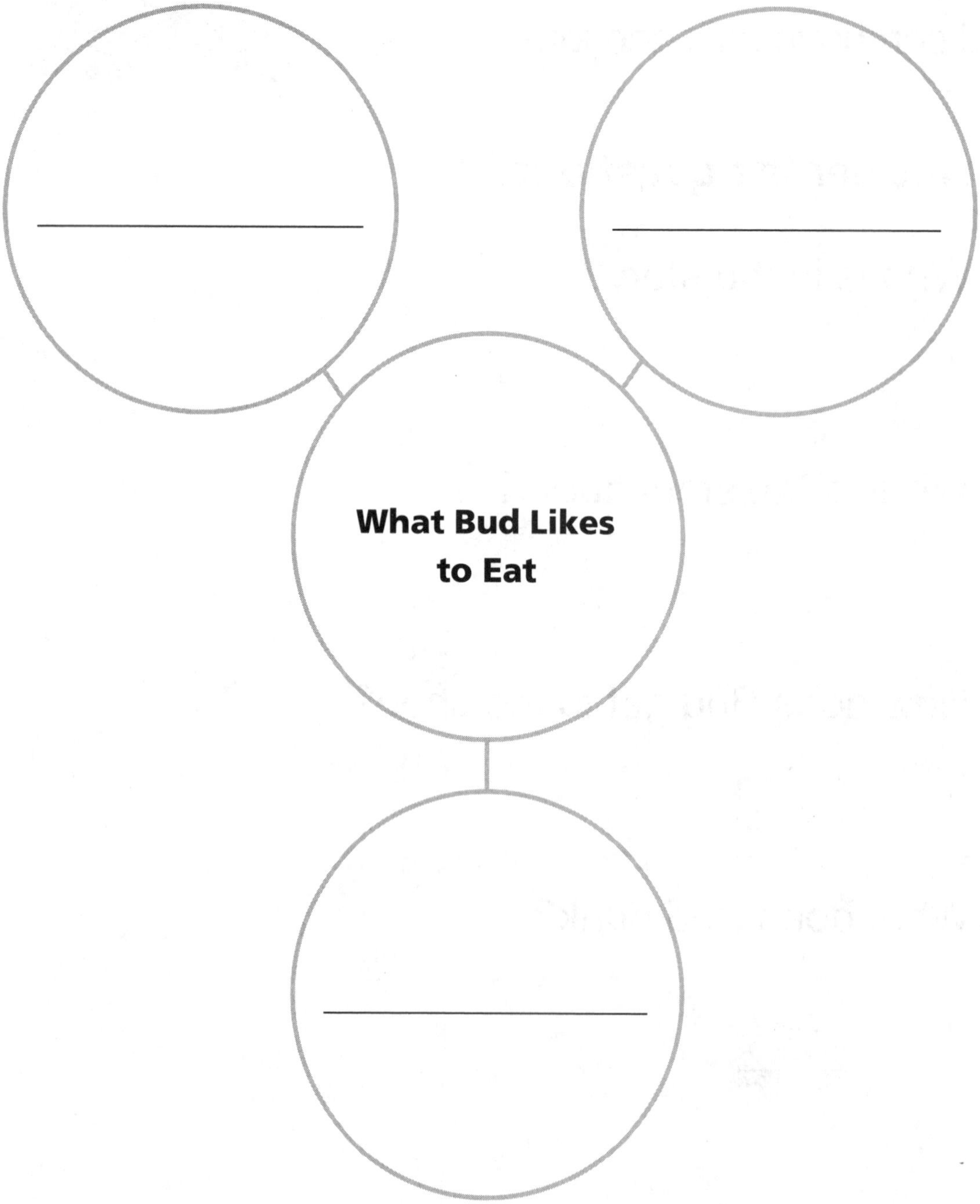

(_____)

(_____)

(**What Bud Likes to Eat**)

(_____)

Name _____ Date _____

Grammar

The pronouns *my, your, her, his, their,* and *our* show who owns something.

You can also use a **name + 's: Kim's ball.**

Write the correct word. Then write the sentence.

Example: (we) That is <u>our</u> doll.

1. (she) This is _____ kite.

_____

_____

2. (Maya) That is _____ backpack.

_____

_____

3. (they) This is _____ cat.

_____

_____

4. (I) That is _____ ball.

_____

_____

Writing

Write the sentences. Use capital letters on words that need them.

Example: This is jo's cat.

<u>This is Jo's cat.</u>

1. That is dan's mom.

_____

- -

_____

2. This is jin's bike.

_____

- -

_____

3. That is may's book.

_____

- -

_____

4. This is pat's pencil.

_____

- -

_____

5. It is anna's ball.

_____

- -

_____

Name _____ Date _____

Vocabulary

A. **Fill in the missing letter to complete the word.**

Sight Words	
use	
this	
be	

1. t ____ is

4. doct ____ r

2. ____ e

5. us ____

3. m ____ il

Story Words
doctor
mail

B. **Write the word that completes each sentence.**

6. I put the _____ in the box.

7. What do you want to _____ when you are big?

8. The _____ can help you get well.

9. That ball is new and _____ ball is old.

10. May I _____ Mom's mug?

Phonics

A. Circle the word with the long
a sound.

1. late   at   pal

2. that   name   ad

3. made   mad   am

4. ate   had   sat

B. Write the letter that stands for the sound at
the *beginning* of the word.

5.   _____

6.   _____

7.   _____

8.   _____

Name _____ Date _____

Think It Over

Reread to tell about the story.

Jane can hand mail to Doctor Ron.

Doctor Ron helps pets get well.

Doctor Ron can use this mail. It will

help sick cats and dogs get well.

A. Answer the questions.

1. Who is the story about?

The story is about _____ .

2. How does Jane help people?

Jane takes _____ to people.

3. Why does Doctor Ron look happy?

Dr. Ron is happy to get his _____ .

B. Think about the story. It tells about four things that Jane does. Look at the pictures. Write *a*, *b*, *c*, and *d* to show the right order.

4. _____

5. _____

6. _____

7. _____

Name _____ Date _____

Grammar

> Use **will + verb** to talk about things that will happen in the future.
>
> Use **will not** for things that are not going to happen. **will not = won't**

Write will or will not to complete each sentence.

Example: <u>Will</u> you play soccer? Yes, I <u>will</u>.

1. _____ she go to the pool?

Yes, she _____.

2. _____ he play at the park?

No, he _____.

3. _____ her sister run?

Yes, she _____.

4. _____ you get the mail?

No, I _____.

5. _____ he eat a snack?

No, he _____.

Writing

Circle the word *I* in each sentence.

Rewrite the sentence. Write *I* with a capital letter.

Example: i will play soccer.

I will play soccer.

1. i will go to the pool.

_____

2. i will call my mom.

_____

3. No, i will not get the paper.

_____

4. Yes, i will use a computer.

_____

Name _____ Date _____

Review

Answer the questions after reading Unit 2. You can go back and reread to help find the answers.

1. In *People Can Help*, how can Ed help people? Circle the letter of the right answer.

   a. He can sit down and rest.
   b. He can take mail to people.
   c. He can take people on a bus.
   d. He can help get books for people.

2. Circle all the words with the short *o* sound.

   > Dot has a good job. She put mail on top of the box.

3. Who can help Dan's dog Top?

   _____ can help Top.

4. In *Bud and His Dad*, how do Bud and Dad get from shop to shop?

   _____

   _____

5. In *Bud and His Dad*, what is Bud's *blue* snack? Circle the letter of the right answer.

    a. ice cream   **c.** jam

    b. milk   **d.** a bun

6. In *Jane Has a Job*, what does Doctor Ron get from Jane?

_____

_____

_____

_____

7. Circle all the words with the long *a* sound.

Jane can take a cake to Nate.

8. In *Jane Has a Job*, who sends a letter to Rob? Circle the letter of the right answer.

    a. Doctor Ron   **c.** Wes

    b. Jane   **d.** Rob

9. You read about many kinds of jobs in this unit. How are all the jobs alike?

All the jobs help _____ .

Name _____ Date _____

Writing Workshop

Write a Letter

You will write a letter to a friend. Tell your friend what you do at school.

> May 3, 2011
>
> Dear Maria,
>   How are you? What do you do at school?
> I read books. We sing. Today I will use a
> computer.
>   Your friend,
>   May

1. Prewrite What do you do at school? Write a list.

Things I Do at School

_____

_____

_____

_____

_____

2. Draft Write a letter. Use the ideas in your list.

_____

Dear _____

How are you? Today I will

_____

_____

_____

_____

Your friend,

_____

3 & 4. Revise and Edit Look for errors in your letter. Correct the errors to make your writing better. Go to page 50 of the Student Book and use the Editing Checklist.

5. Publish Make a clean copy of your letter on a separate sheet of paper. Share it with the class.

Name _____ Date _____

Fluency

A. Listen to the words in each row. Which word sounds different? Circle it. Read each row of words aloud.

1. dog   doll   frog   old

2. blue   bug   cup   jug

3. cake   gate   five   plane

B. Listen. Then write the words with the same sounds in the right boxes.

bunny   bus   flame   hot   plate   pot

Unit 2

C. Take turns reading the sentences aloud with a partner. Use your finger to follow the words.

> He is Doctor Ron.

> My new pet is a bunny.

> The plane is big.

D. Read the sentences in Part C again. Draw a line from each sentence to the correct picture.

Name _____ Date _____

Learning Checklist

Phonics

☐ Short *o: c, h*
☐ Short *u: b, j*
☐ Long *a; r, w*

Strategies

☐ Prior Knowledge
☐ Main Idea
☐ Sequence

Grammar

☐ *Can* + Verb
☐ Possessive Pronouns
☐ *Will* + Verb

Writing

☐ Draw a picture of things you can do. Write about them.
☐ Draw a picture of something that belongs to a friend. Write about it.
☐ Draw a picture of three things you will do this weekend. Write about them.
☐ Writing Workshop: Write a Letter

Listening and Speaking

☐ Tell a Story about a Fun Thing You Do

Name _____ Date _____

Vocabulary

A. **Write the word that completes each sentence.**

Sight Words

of

to

green

1. Most frogs are _____ .

2. I dress up in my fun

   _____ .

3. I like _____ put it on.

4. We waved flags at the

   _____ .

5. We have lots _____ fun.

Story Words

carnival

celebration

costume

B. **Find a word in the letters. Write the word you find.**

6. v c a r n i v a l a   _____

7. p u o f o u a l c   _____

8. l m g r e e n v a l   _____

9. p c o s t u m e l p   _____

Unit 3

Phonics

A. Circle the word that names the picture.

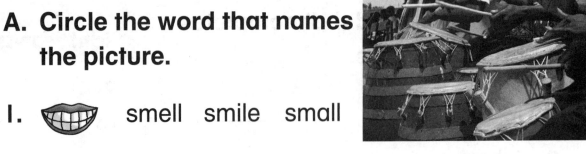

1. smell   smile   small

2. nine   nip   note

3. milk   make   mice

4. five   fill   for

B. Write the letter that stands for the missing sound.

5. di ____ e

6. fo ____

7. a ____

Name _____ Date _____

Think It Over

Reread to tell about the story.

I can have a fun time at a carnival.

I can put on a big blue wig and a mask to hide.

I can smile and dress up.

A. Answer the questions.

1. What is your favorite celebration?

   My favorite celebration is _____ .

2. Why do people wear masks?

   People wear masks to _____ .

3. When do you wear a costume?

   I wear a costume when _____ .

B. Fill in the diagram to compare and contrast Carnival and July 4 celebrations. Put things that are the same in the middle. Put things that are different on one side or the other.

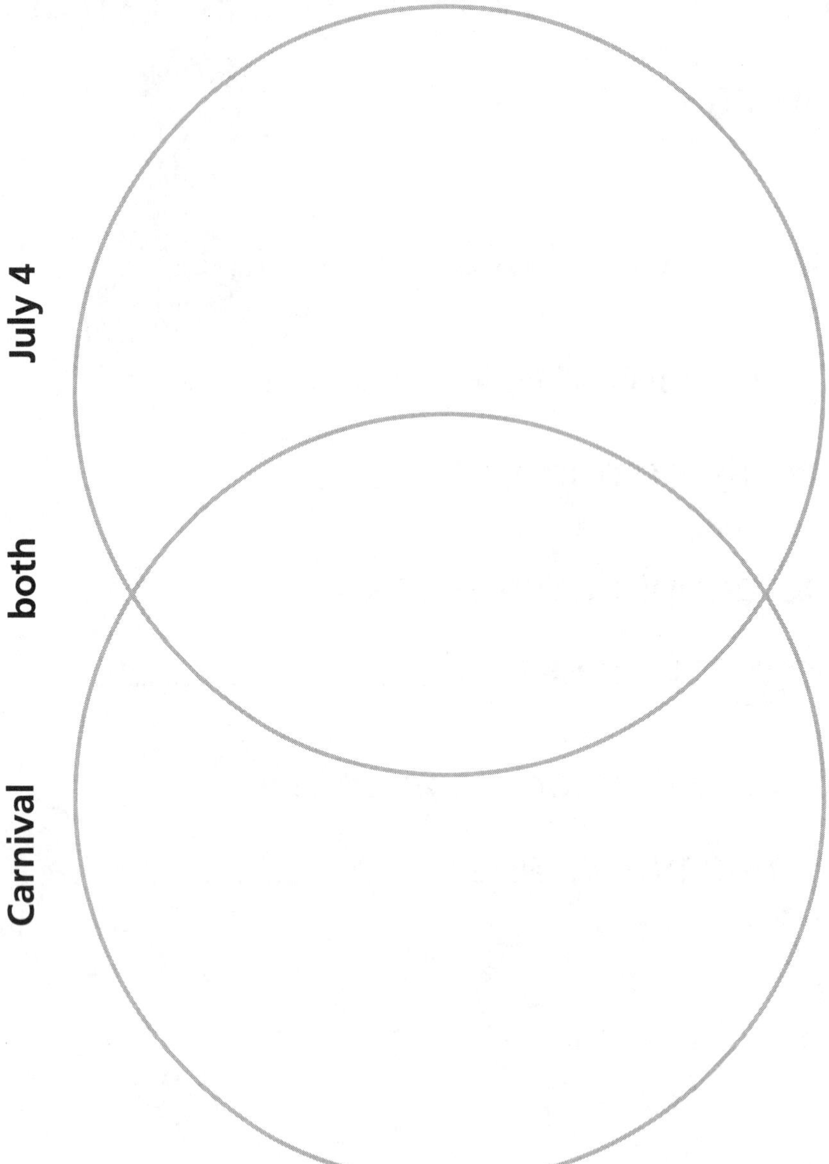

July 4

both

Carnival

Name _____ Date _____

Grammar

Use verbs with **-ing** to talk about what you are doing right now.

Use **am, is,** or **are** before the verb.

Find the word in the box to complete the sentence.

Add **-ing** to the word. Write the word in the sentence.

catch play watch kick draw

Example: He is <u>jumping</u> rope.

1. My dog is _____ the ball.

2. Are you _____ a movie?

3. He is _____ the ball.

4. The girls are _____ a frog.

5. We are _____ basketball.

Writing

Read the paragraph. It is missing four periods. Add the periods.

I am playing ball with my dog I am

throwing the ball My dog is catching it

My dog is fun

Name _____ Date _____

Vocabulary

A. Write the word that completes each sentence.

Sight Words
first
then
with

1. We are riding a _____ over the snow.

2. Lil runs fast and gets home _____ .

3. There is no school on _____ .

4. I am eating a snack _____ Jan and Jake.

Story Words
Thanksgiving
parade
sleigh

5. We plan to see the big _____ .

B. Fill in the missing letter to complete the word.

6. ____ arade

7. firs ____

8. slei ____ h

9. Th ____ nksgiving

10. t ____ en

61

Phonics

A. Circle the word with the long *u* sound.

1. cub   but   cute

2. use   tub   tab

3. cube   code   bud

4. run   mule   male

B. Write the letter or letters that stand for the sound at the end of the word.

5.   _____

6.   _____

7.   _____

8.   _____

Name _____ Date _____

Think It Over

Reread to tell about the story.

A big parade will pass us by.

I gaze at a big star up in the sky.

Then I see big pipes and a drum.

I sing a tune. I hum and hum.

A. Answer the questions.

1. The star has a big smile. Tell why.

   The star _____ .

2. What does Zack give Sam?

   Zack gives Sam a plate of yams.

   _____ .

3. Why do people go to a parade?

   People go to a parade because

   _____ .

B. Fill in the T-chart. Tell how the people in this story celebrate Thanksgiving with food. Tell what other things they do to celebrate.

Thanksgiving	
with food	**other ways to celebrate**
_____	_____
_____	_____
_____	_____

Name _____ Date _____

Grammar

An **adjective** describes a noun or pronoun.

An adjective can come *before* a *noun*.

An adjective can come after *is*, *am*, or *are*.

Choose an adjective from the list to complete the sentence.

Example: I have a <u>green</u> <u>shirt</u>.

long	curly	big	white	blue

1. He has _____ eyes.

2. Her hair is _____.

3. My shirt is _____.

4. He has _____ pants.

5. She has a _____ bookbag.

Writing

Read the sentences. Write the correct word on the line.

1. Ana and Ted _____ (is, are) friends.

2. Ana's hair _____ (is, are) long.

3. Ted's hair _____ (is, are) short.

4. Their eyes _____ (is, are) blue.

5. She _____ (is, are) happy.

6. They _____ (is, are) glad.

7. Ted _____ (is, are) standing.

8. They _____ (is, are) both standing.

Name _____ Date _____

Vocabulary

A. Fill in the missing letters to complete the word.

1. sch _____

2. _____ ite

3. o _____

4. _____ on

5. bl _____

Sight Words

white

blue

our

Story Words

America

moon

school

B. Draw a line from each word to the sentence that tells about it.

6. blue

a. This is the color of snow.

7. America

b. This is a country.

8. school

c. This is a place where kids go to learn.

9. white

d. This is the color of the sky on a nice day.

Phonics

A. Write the letter that stands for the sound at the *beginning* of the word.

1.  ____

2. ____

3.  ____

4.  ____

B. Circle the word with the long *o* sound.

5. hop   hope   hot

6. note   not   nap

7. cane   cone   can

8. rod   rode   rob

Name _____ Date _____

Think It Over

Reread to tell about the story.

The American flag is red, white, and blue.

America is our home.

A. Complete the sentences or answer the questions.

1. The American flag is red, white, and

_____ .

2. _____ is the name of the country

where we live.

3. What is on the American flag?

_____

B. Think of words to tell about America's flag. Write the words on the lines below.

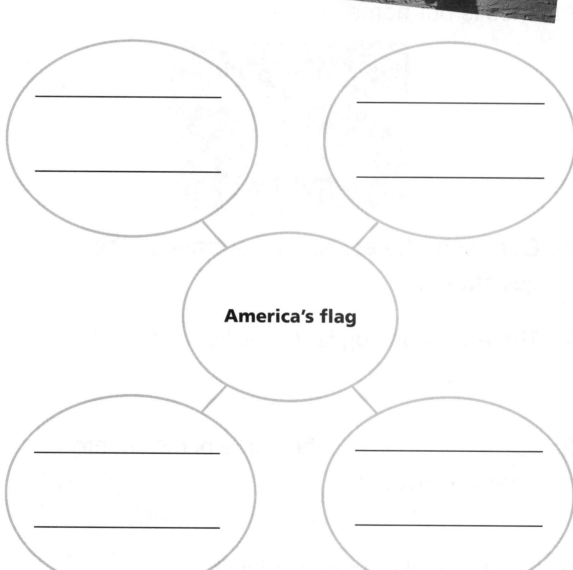

America's flag

Name _____ Date _____

Grammar

Use the **simple present** for things that happen again and again or are always true.

For **he, she,** or **it,** add –s after the verb.

Write the correct simple present verb for each sentence.

Example: (dive) She <u>dives</u> in the pool.

1. (play)   He _____ at the beach.

2. (jump)   They _____ rope.

3. (make)   She _____ a sandcastle.

4. (draw)   They _____ a picture.

5. (sing)   She _____ today.

Writing

Read the sentences. Write the correct word on the line.

1. We _____ (play, plays) soccer at school.

2. The ball _____ (is, are) black and white.

3. We _____ (kick, kicks) the ball.

4. We _____ (throw, throws) the ball, too.

5. We _____ (run, runs) fast.

6. She _____ (run, runs) faster.

7. Soccer _____ (is, are) fun.

8. We _____ (is, are) good.

Name _____ Date _____

Review

Answer the questions after reading Unit 3. You can go back and reread to help find the answers.

1. In *Celebration Time!*, what can the new year be named for? Circle the letter of the right answer.

    a. an ox   **c.** a joke

    b. a place   **d.** a game

2. Circle all the action verbs.

> In Ghana, tribes plant crops. Drums tap. People celebrate.

3. Finish this sentence about *Thanksgiving Time!*

Thanksgiving Time! tells about

_____

- .

4. In *Thanksgiving Time!*, what does the family do at the end of Thanksgiving? Circle the letter of the right answer.

  a. The family sees a big parade.
  b. The family makes a home in a new land.
  c. The family sees a big Thanksgiving game.
  d. The family takes a fun sleigh ride.

5. *A Flag* tells about the American and Texan flags. Name three places where you can see these flags.

I can see a flag _____ ,

_____ , and _____ .

6. Circle all the words with the long *o* sound.

The man poked a hole in the moon to put up the flag pole.

7. What is America's flag like? Circle the letter of the *correct* answer.

  a. It is big and round.
  b. It is red, white, and blue.
  c. It is white, red, and green.
  d. It is new and little.

Name _____ Date _____

Writing Workshop: Write a Descriptive Paragraph

You will write a descriptive paragraph. Here is Dan's paragraph.

I like the park. The trees are tall and green. My dad and I play soccer. My dog and I play with a ball.

1. Prewrite What place do you like? Fill in the web with descriptions of different things you like about the place.

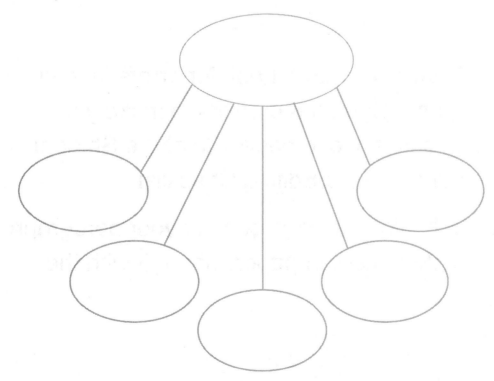

2. **Draft** Write a descriptive paragraph. Use the ideas in your web.

_____

_____

_____

_____

_____

_____

_____

_____

_____

_____

3 & 4. **Revise and Edit** Look for errors in your paragraph. Correct the errors to make your writing better. Go to page 170 of the Student Book and use the Editing Checklist.

5. **Publish** Make a clean copy of your paragraph on another sheet of paper. Share it with the class.

Name _____ Date _____

Fluency

A. Listen to the words in each row. Which word is sounds different? Circle it. Read each row of words aloud.

1. bike   five   little   ride

2. bug   cube   mule   use

3. bowl   cow   hole   poke

B. Listen. Then write the words with the same sounds in the correct boxes.

community   fire   music   nine   pole   stove

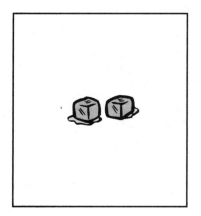

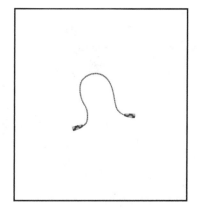

C. Take turns reading the sentences with a partner. Use your finger to follow the words.

I have five white birds.

The truck is very old.

Joe has a red rose.

D. Read the sentences in Part C again. Draw a line from each sentence to the correct picture.

Name _____ Date _____

Learning Checklist

Phonics

☐ Long *i: v, x*
☐ Long *u: k, ck*
☐ Long *o: g, z*

Strategies

☐ Compare and Contrast
☐ Summarize
☐ Context Clues

Grammar

☐ Verbs with *-ing*
☐ Adjectives
☐ Simple Present Tense: Statements

Writing

☐ Draw a picture of you doing your favorite activity. Write about your picture.
☐ Draw a picture of you. Describe yourself.
☐ Draw a picture of things you do in the summer. Describe them.
☐ Writing Workshop: Write a Descriptive Paragraph

Listening and Speaking

☐ Description Guessing Game

Name _____ Date _____

Vocabulary

A. Write the word that completes each sentence.

1. How did that tree grow

   _____ tall?

2. Mom looked _____ of

   the window.

3. I am happy _____ you

   are my friend.

4. It is fun to get down and

   _____ like a duck.

Sight Words

why

because

so

out

Story Words

waddle

duckling

feathers

B. Circle four vocabulary words in the Word Search.

U	D	U	C	K	L	I	N	G
B	E	C	A	U	S	E	J	P
W	H	Y	I	H	G	E	V	M
I	F	E	A	T	H	E	R	S

Phonics

A. Circle five words with the long *e* sound.

> Reed sees a seal swim in
> the green sea.

B. Circle the letters that stand for the sound at the beginning of the word.

1.		th	ch	sh
2.		ch	wh	th
3.		sh	ch	ph
4.		sh	th	wh
5.		ch	th	sh

Name _____ Date _____

Think It Over

Reread to tell about the story.

I see a duck. Why is it so small?

It is so small because it just hatched.

An egg shell cracks. I see feet! I see a beak!

A duckling can get out of its shell.

A. Answer the questions.

1. What does *hatched* mean?

   Hatched means _____ .

2. What parts of the duck can I see just after the
   egg cracks?

   I can see _____ .

3. Circle the words with the long *e* sound.

   I see a beak.

B. Look at the pictures in *Little Duck*. Use the pictures to predict what happens. Write your predictions on the left side of the chart. Then reread the story. Fill in the right side of the chart.

My Predictions	What Happens
I think the duckling will:	The duckling:
_____	_____
_____	_____
_____	_____
_____	_____
_____	_____
_____	_____

Name _____ Date _____

Grammar

To make questions with the simple present, use
what, when, and *where* + **do** + subject + verb.

**Circle the word to complete the question. Write
the word.**

Example: Where (do, does) you shop?

1. When _____ you watch a movie?
   (do does)

2. Where _____ he use the computer?
   (do does)

3. What _____ he do at the park?
   (do does)

4. When _____ she go to sleep?
   (do does)

5. Where _____ you play soccer?
   (do does)

Writing

Read the conversation. Write the correct word on the line.

Student 1: What do you do on the weekend?

Student 2: I _____ (get, gets) up late.

Next, I _____ (play, plays) with my cat.

Then we _____ (shop, shops). After that,

I _____ (ride, rides) my bicycle.

Name _____ Date _____

Vocabulary

A. Write the word that completes each sentence.

1. It takes time to _____ tall.

2. I did not know you at all

_____ we met.

3. The letter *b* comes

_____ the letter *a*.

4. A little bud can turn into a

_____ .

B. Draw a line from each word to the sentence that tells about it.

5. water   a. This means a time later on.

6. grow   b. Seas and lakes have lots of it.

7. pumpkin   c. This means to get big.

8. after   d. This is round and orange.

Phonics

A. Circle the words in each sentence with the long *a* sound.

1. I aim to help you find your way.

2. It took all day to get to the bay.

3. I made a gray duck with feathers.

4. I ate ten seeds near the bay.

5. We had to wait to pay for our snack.

B. Say the words on the left. Think of how the underlined letters sound. Then draw a line to the word on the right that has the same sound.

6. r<u>ai</u>n   way

7. <u>th</u>at   you

8. <u>y</u>arn   thump

Name _____ Date _____

Think It Over

Reread to tell about the story.

This seed is named a pit or a stone.

It may grow to be a peach tree.

It will need a lot of water and sun to help it grow.

A peach grows on a tree.

A. Answer the questions.

1. What is a peach pit?

   A peach pit is a _____.

2. What does a peach pit need to grow?

   A peach pit needs _____.

3. Where do peaches grow?

   Peaches grow _____.

B. Reread the story. Think about the main idea. Then complete the chart.

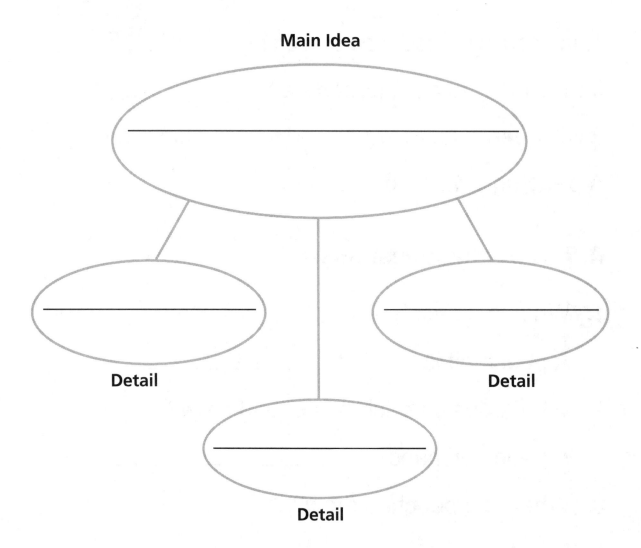

Main Idea

Detail

Detail

Detail

Name _____ Date _____

Grammar

You can use words like *first, next, then, after, after that*, and *finally* to tell steps to do something or to tell the time in order.

Choose words from the box to tell about how kittens become cats. Write the word in each sentence.

first   next   then   after   after that   finally

Example: <u>First,</u> the kittens are born.

1. _____, the kittens are little.

2. _____, they eat.

3. _____, they grow and play.

4. _____, they become cats.

Writing

Read the paragraph. It is missing four periods. Add the periods.

First, you plant a seed Then you

water it After that, you will see a blossom

Finally, you will see a big plant

Name _____ Date _____

Vocabulary

A. Fill in the missing letters to complete the word.

1. ____ a t

2. a n i ____ a ____ s

3. a l ____

4. m ____ n ____

5. f o o ____ c h a ____ n

Sight Words
many
they
all
eat

Sight Words
animals
birds
food chain

B. Write the word that completes each sentence.

6. Will _____ get up early?

7. She will _____ a snack.

8. Do _____ animals need food?

9. Some _____ have brown fur.

10. Plants are part of the _____ _____.

11. _____ people have blue eyes.

12. Do _____ fly?

Phonics

A. Circle the word with the long *i* sound.

1. rig   rip   right

2. wild   wig   wit

3. spy   hay   toy

4. fit   fight   fish

5. trim   tray   try

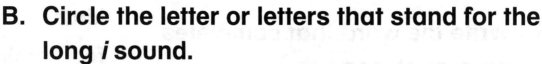

B. Circle the letter or letters that stand for the long *i* sound.

6. sky

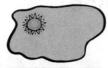

7. right

8. fly

9. child

10. light

Name _____ Date _____

Think It Over

Reread to tell about the story.

Gray foxes can climb trees.

Then they can look for food.

The birds fly away

because the fox climbs the tree.

A. Answer the questions.

1. Who can climb trees?

   Gray _____ climb trees.

2. What do gray foxes look for?

   Gray foxes look for _____.

3. Why do birds fly away?

   The fox climbs the _____.

B. Look at the pictures. Fill in the chart with words that name animals that live in the United States.

bird   bat   fox   goat   fish

Animals That Live in the United States

Then draw a picture of one of the animals.

Name _____ Date _____

Grammar

Singular nouns name one person, place, or thing.

Plural nouns name more than one person, place, or thing. We usually add **-s** to make nouns plural.

Write each noun in the box in the correct list.

paper doll kites pens shirt friend dogs tigers

Example: <u>Singular</u>   <u>Plural</u>
              animal   bikes

Singular (one)	Plural (more than one)
_____	_____
_____	_____
_____	_____
_____	_____

Writing

Read the paragraph. Write the correct word on the line.

All animals _____ (need, needs) food.

A fox _____ (live, lives) in the woods.

It _____ (hunt, hunts) for food. A gray

fox _____ (climb, climbs) a tree. It

_____ (look, looks) for birds to eat.

The birds fly away.

Name _____ Date _____

Review

Answer the questions after reading Unit 4. You can go back and reread to help find the answers.

1. In *Little Duck*, what are new ducks called? Circle the letter of the right answer.

   a. peeps   **c.** ducklings
   b. eggs   **d.** waddles

2. How many animals are in *Animals*? Which animal is your favorite? Why?

   _____

   _____

   _____

   _____

3. What do ducks do so they can swim?

   _____

   _____

   _____

   _____

4. In *Plants*, what do seeds need to grow? Circle the letter of the right answer.

   a. soft ground

   b. vines and blossoms

   c. peaches and pumpkins

   d. water and sun

5. Circle the words with the long *a* sound.

Rain will make the plants grow.

6. Read the sentences. Then use words from the box to show the order.

| Finally | First | Next | Then |

   a. _____ the egg shell cracks.

   b. _____ the duckling's feet come out.

   c. _____ you can see the whole duckling.

   d. _____ the duckling can stand up!

Name _____ Date _____

Writing Workshop: Write an Expository Paragraph

You will write an expository paragraph. Read Julio's paragraph about a pet.

My favorite pet is a dog. Dogs can be big or little. A dog likes to play. A dog likes to walk in the park. A dog can be a good friend.

1. Prewrite Think of a pet that you would like to have. Write facts about the pet in the web.

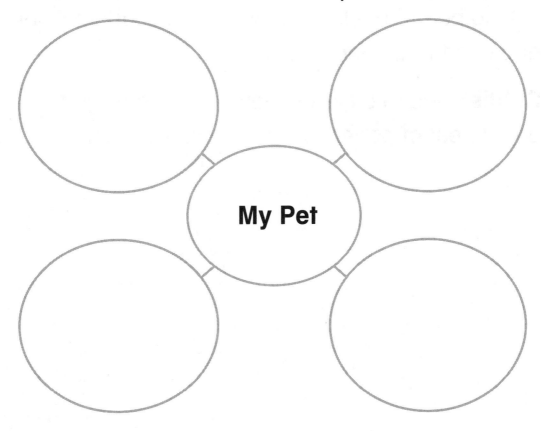

2. **Draft** Write an expository paragraph on the lines. Use the ideas from your word web.

_____

- -

_____

_____

- -

_____

_____

- -

_____

_____

- -

_____

3 & 4. **Revise and Edit** Look for errors in your paragraph. Correct the errors to make your writing better. Go to page 58 of the Student Book and use the Editing Checklist.

5. **Publish** Make a clean copy of your paragraph on a sheet of paper. Share it with the class.

Name _____ Date _____

Fluency

A. Listen to the words in each row. Which word sounds different? Circle it. Read each row of words aloud.

1. beak   eye   feet   read

2. bath   plane   snail   train

3. child   fly   night   pig

B. Listen. Then write the words in the right boxes.

cake   cry   green   mail   sheep   sign

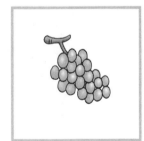

C. Take turns reading the sentences aloud with a partner. Use your finger to follow the words.

I see my cat in the tree.

We will have rain today.

I want to fly my kite.

D. Read the sentences in Part C again. Draw a line from each sentence to the correct picture.

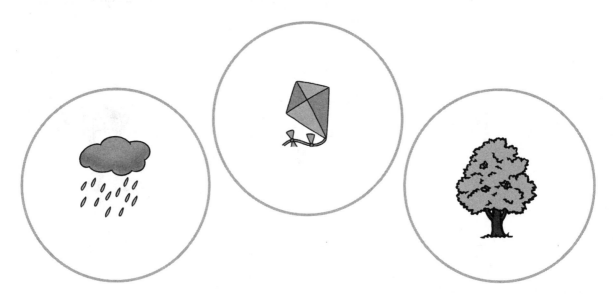

Name _____ Date _____

Learning Checklist
Word Study and Phonics

☐ Long e: *ch, sh*
☐ Long a: *th, y*
☐ Long *i*

Strategies

☐ Predict
☐ Predict
☐ Cause and Effect

Grammar

☐ Simple Present Tense: Questions
☐ Time Order Words
☐ Nouns: Singular and Plural

Writing

☐ Draw a picture. Write about the things you do after school.
☐ Draw a picture of a plant you like. Then write about how it grows.
☐ Draw a picture of an animal you like. Write about it.
☐ Writing Workshop: Write an Expository Paragraph

Listening and Speaking

☐ Explain How to Do Something

Name _____ Date _____

Vocabulary

A. Write the word that completes each sentence.

Sight Words

one

two

wants

from

1. I lost a mitten and have just

_____ left.

2. This note is _____ Lee.

3. He ate _____ eggs.

4. Shep _____ to go

outside.

Story Words

bought

soccer

ball

5. My favorite sport is

_____ .

B. Circle the vocabulary words.

6. Marco bought one soccer ball.

7. Harry bought two apples from the store.

8. We bought lunch from the shop.

Phonics

A. Circle the word with the long *o* sound.

1. for   fox   flow

2. soap   shop   sock

3. dog   dot   doe

B. Write the word that names the picture. Circle the letter pair that stands for the long *o* sound.

4. _____

5. _____

6.  _____

Name _____ Date _____

Think It Over

Reread to tell about the story.

Blake likes to play in a football game.

Blake can throw and pass.

Joan can run fast. Cliff can kick the football.

Blake needs one more kid. Then they can play a game.

A. Answer the questions.

1. Why does Blake need one more kid?

Blake needs one more kid so

_____ .

2. How many kids will play the game?

_____ kids will play.

3. Circle the word with the same sound
you hear in *home*.

Blake can throw and pass.

B. Fill in the diagram to compare and contrast a football and a soccer ball. Put things that are the same in the middle. Put things that are not the same on one side or the other.

football   both   soccer ball

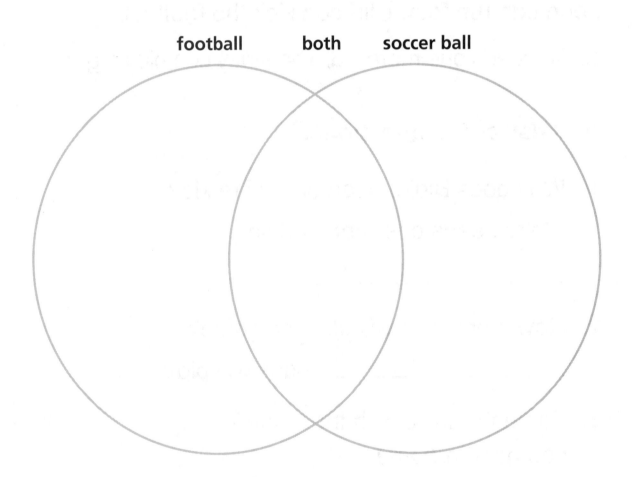

Name _____ Date _____

Grammar

> **Proper nouns** are names of specific people, places, and things. A proper noun starts with a *capital letter*. Other nouns are **common nouns.**

Underline the nouns in each sentence. Write each noun in the correct list.

Example: <u>Stephan</u> rides a <u>bike</u>.

1. Jose has a new puppy.

2. Lola likes her red shirt and pants.

3. Do you like New York?

Proper Nouns	Common Nouns
Stephan	bike
_____	_____
_____	_____
_____	_____

Writing

Read the paragraph. Circle each proper noun that needs a capital letter. Write the proper nouns in the list below.

My friend is (ava). We like to go to long beach. We swim and dive. My friend felix likes the brookfield zoo. We see tigers and lions.

Proper Nouns

Ava

1. _____

2. _____

3. _____

Name _____ Date _____

Vocabulary

A. **Write the letters in the right order to make a word.**

1. e i l v _____

2. i b g _____

3. p a l y _____

4. t b e s _____

5. l l o c e _____

6. o r w l d _____

7. k o w n _____

Sight Words
best
know
live
big

Story Words
cello
world
play

B. **Write the word that completes each sentence.**

8. Dan wants to _____ how to swim.

9. The family wants to _____ in America.

10. Yo-Yo-Ma likes to _____ the _____ .

Phonics

A. Circle the word with the same vowel sound as *cow*.

1. town   two   tone

2. land   pond   round

3. hoe   how   who

B. Circle the word that names the picture.

4. I was a whale in the play.

5. We see the wheel on the car.

6. Where should I go?

Name _____ Date _____

Think It Over

Reread to tell about the story.

The cello is big.

But Yo-Yo Ma was a small boy.

One day, his dad made a cello

for him.

It was still too big.

Yo-Yo had to sit on big books to play his cello!

Answer the questions.

I. Yo-Yo wanted to play the _____.

2. His cello was too _____.

3. Yo-Yo had to sit on _____ to play
the cello.

Learning Strategies

Read the sentences in each column.
Add words about the story.

K – What I Know	W – What I Want to Know	L – What I Learned
I know that a cello is _____ _____ _____.	I want to know how Yo-Yo's dad can help _____ _____ _____.	I learned that his dad _____ _____ _____.
I know that Yo-Yo was _____ _____ _____.		I learned that Yo-Yo sat on _____ _____ _____.

Name _____ Date _____

Grammar

Use **was** with *I, he, she,* and *it.*
Use **were** with *we, you,* and *they.*
To make questions, use **was** or **were** + subject.
You can also use **who, what, where, why,
when,** and **how** to ask questions.

Use *was* or *were* to complete each sentence.

Example: Where <u>was</u> dad?

He <u>was</u> at the store.

1. Where _____ you?

   I _____ at the playground.

2. Who _____ with you?

   My friend _____ there.

3. Why _____ you there?

   We _____ playing baseball.

4. _____ it fun?

   It _____ fun to play.

Writing

Read the paragraphs. Write the correct word on the line.

I _____ (was, were) happy last weekend.

We _____ (was, were) at the zoo.

The tiger _____ (was, were) big. The

lion _____ (was, were) the best. We

_____ (was, were) sad when we left.

    I _____ (was, were) five last year.

My sister _____ (was, were) four.

We _____ (was, were) at camp.

The days _____ (was, were) sunny.

It _____ (was, were) warm.

Name _____ Date _____

Vocabulary

A. Write the word that completes each sentence.

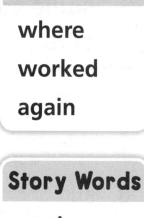

Sight Words

where

worked

again

Story Words

cattle

horse

1. Let's look at this

    book _____ .

2. Jane rode a _____
   to school!

3. A lot of _____ went
   out to the field to eat.

4. Do you know _____ my hat is?

5. I am tired because I _____ hard all day.

B. Draw a picture that tells about the sentence.

We are riding the horse.

Phonics

A. Circle the word with the same sound as the *ue* in *clue*.

I. give   grow   glue

2. cool   cup   can

3. suit   sit   seat

B. Circle the word with the same sound as the *ue* in *clue*.

4. We have a new kite.

5. The wind blew the leaves.

6. I like to eat fruit.

7. I have a blue sheet on my bed.

8 I used glue on my project.

Name _____ Date _____

Think It Over

Reread to tell about the story.

Cowboys in the United States herded cattle to big ranches. Cowboys had to help cattle cross cold, wet streams. They had to help cattle stay safe. Cowboys are still strong.

A. Answer the questions.

1. Where did cowboys take cattle?

   Cowboys took cattle _____.

2. Circle another word for *herded*.

   a. left   **c.** moved
   b. sold   **d.** kept

3. How did cowboys help cattle?

   _____

   _____

   _____

   _____

B. Fill in the T-chart. Compare and contrast a cowboy's life and your life.

Different Lives	
A Cowboy's Life	**My Life**
_____	_____
_____	_____
_____	_____
_____	_____
_____	_____
_____	_____

Name _____ Date _____

Grammar

> To form the **simple past**, add *-ed*
> to most regular verbs.
> Some verbs are irregular in the simple past, such
> as *ate, came, did, had, left, made, saw, went*.

Change the verb to the simple past.
Write the verb in the sentence.

Example: (work) I <u>worked</u> at school.

1. (play)   We _____ at the beach

2. (call)   Ava _____ her mom.

3. (come) We _____ to school.

4. (kick)   The dog _____ the ball.

5. (watch) My sister _____ the movie.

Writing

Read the paragraph. It is missing six periods. Add the periods.

It rained and rained We had to stay inside We watched a movie We listened to music Then we had dinner After that we did homework

Name _____ Date _____

Review

**Answer the questions after reading Unit 5.
You can go back and reread to help find the
answers.**

1. In *One, Two, Three, Play!*, Blake has
one name for the ball in the picture,
and Joe has a different name for it.
List the two names for this ball.

_____

_____

2. Write two sentences about Yo-Yo Ma.

3. Where does Yo-Yo Ma live and how many
children does he have?

4. Where were you yesterday?

_____

5. Circle the words with the same vowel sound as in *out*.

> Our cow is brown and white.

6. In *A Cowboy's Life,* what foods do cowboys eat? Do they work hard?

_____

_____

_____

_____

7. Why is a cowboy hat shaped like this?

_____

_____

_____

_____

Name _____ Date _____

Writing Workshop: Write a Narrative

You will write a narrative. Read Dan's narrative.

Last night, I was outside with my dad. It was dark. We saw an animal. It looked like a dog. Then smaller animals followed it. They were babies. It was a raccoon family!

1. **Prewrite** Think of something interesting that really happened to you. Write your ideas in this story map.

Beginning

↓

Middle

↓

End

2. **Draft** Write a narrative on the lines. Use the ideas from your story map.

_____

_____

_____

_____

_____

_____

_____

_____

3 & 4. **Revise and Edit** Look for errors in your story. Correct the errors to make your writing better. Go to page 118 of the Student Book and use the Editing Checklist.

5. **Publish** Make a clean copy of your narrative on a sheet of paper. Share it with the class.

Name _____ Date _____

Fluency

A. Take turns reading the sentences aloud with a partner. Use your finger to follow the words.

> Put the rope on the goat.

> My new house is brown.

> He wants some new boots.

B. Read the sentences in Part A again. Draw a line from each sentence to the correct picture.

Unit 5

C. Listen to the sentences. Use your finger to follow the words. Read aloud for one minute. Count your words.

A Cowboy's Life tells about the	6
life of cowboys and cowgirls in the	13
past. They worked hard. They herded	19
cattle to and from ranches. Cowboys	25
had big hats and strong ropes, and	32
they rode big horses. We still see	39
cowboys today.	41

D. Read to your teacher, friends, or family.

Name _____ Date _____

Learning Checklist

Phonics

- ☐ Long *o*
- ☐ Wh: Vowel Diphthongs
- ☐ Letters: *ue, ui, ew*

Strategies

- ☐ Make Inferences
- ☐ Draw Conclusions
- ☐ Compare and Contrast

Grammar

- ☐ Common and Proper Nouns
- ☐ Past: *Be*
- ☐ Simple Past Tense

Writing

- ☐ Tell a story you know. Draw a picture of it.
- ☐ Write a journal entry. Who were you with? Where were you? Draw a picture.
- ☐ What did you do yesterday? Draw a picture and write.
- ☐ Writing Workshop: Write a Narrative

Listening and Speaking

- ☐ A Skit

Name _____ Date _____

Vocabulary

A. Write the word that completes each sentence.

1. I like to listen to _____ .

2. I play with my _____ .

3. My dad and I read

   _____ .

4. Can you _____ the
   window, please?

5. You can _____ to the park.

Sight Words

together

open

come

Story Words

friends

music

B. Fill in the missing vowels to complete the word.

6. ____ p ____ n

7. c ____ m ____

8. f r ____ ____ n d s

9. t ____ g ____ t h ____ r

10. m ____ s ____ c

Phonics

A. Write *oo* to complete each word. Draw a line to the picture.

1. m ____ n

2. b ____ k

3. f ____ d

4. r ____ f

B. Circle the word with an *oo* sound as in *moon* or *book*.

5. soon   son   9. booth   both

6. boy   boot   10. shook   show

7. toy   tooth   11. chose   cook

8. wood   world   12. zone   zoom

Name _____ Date _____

Think It Over

Reread to tell about the story.

Max and Ray come together to fix a big box. The box is open on top. It has red, blue, and striped balls. Max and Ray will tape its side and fix it up.

A. Answer the questions.

1. What do Max and Ray fix?

May and Ray fix _____ .

2. How do they fix it?

They _____ its side.

3. What do Max and Ray help each other do at school?

Max helps Ray _____ . Ray helps Max _____ .

B. Complete the star with activities Max and Ray do together.

_____

_____   _____

**Max and Ray
have a lot of fun together.**

_____   _____

Name _____   Date _____

Grammar

We use **imperatives** to make commands, give
directions, or tell someone how to do something.
Use the base form of the verb to make an imperative.

**Underline the imperative verb in each sentence.
Write a list of the imperative verbs.**

Example: Put flour in the bowl.

I. Then mix the flour and the sugar.

2. Bake the cookies today.

3. Do your homework.

4. Now, fill the bucket with water.

Imperative Verbs

Put _____

5. _____   7. _____

6. _____   8. _____

Writing

**Read the paragraph. It is missing five periods.
Add the periods.**

I will teach you to make eggs First,

put the eggs in a bowl Next, mix the

eggs Then cook the eggs After that,

eat them

Name _____ Date _____

Vocabulary

A. Write the word that completes each sentence.

1. The _____ is crying.

2. Look _____ the little ducklings.

3. The _____ is a very big animal.

4. The _____ is a slow animal.

5. My friend and I are not the same. We are _____ .

Sight Words
over
baby
different

Story Words
hippopotamus
tortoise

B. Use a word from one of the boxes to write a sentence.

6. _____

_____

_____

139

Phonics

A. Circle the word with the *er, ir,* or *ur* sound.

1. A tortoise does not have fur.

2. The hippopotamus lost his herd.

3. There's a girl in the park.

B. Draw a line to the word that names the picture.

4.   girl

5.   bird

6.   nurse

Name _____ Date _____

Think It Over

Reread to tell about the story.

Meet Owen and Mzee. They are different, but they are family.

Owen is a hippopotamus that has lost his herd. Owen likes to stay close to Mzee. He may think Mzee is like his dad.

A. Answer the questions.

1. What happened to Owen?

_____

_____

2. What does Mzee look like?

_____

_____

3. Why are Mzee and Owen a family?

_____

_____

B. Fill in the Word Web for Mzee and Owen. Write words that describe them inside each circle.

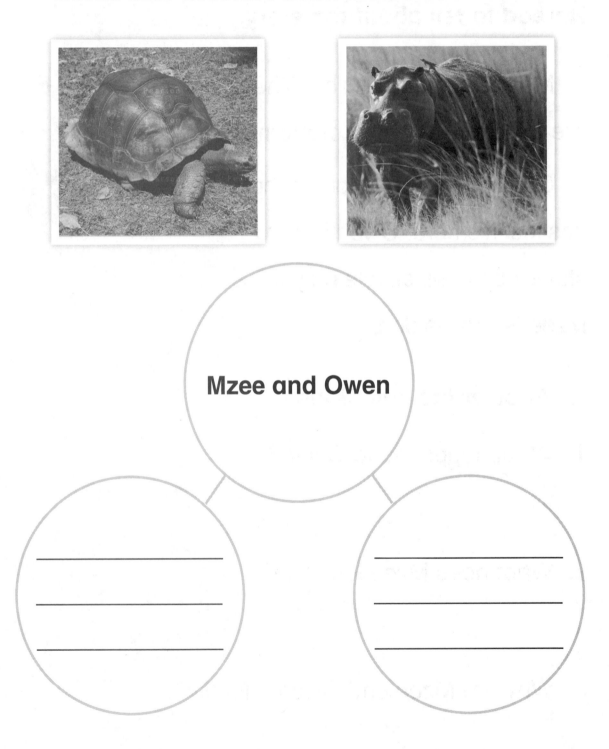

Name _____ Date _____

Grammar

> Use **and** to show plus. You can use **and** to connect two nouns, two verbs, or two adjectives. Use **or** to show a choice.

Circle the correct word to complete the sentence.

Example: The dog is big ((and), or) fast.

1. Kwan (and, or) Mei like to swim.

2. Is the shirt pink (and, or) red?

3. Do you have one (and, or) two cats?

4. I don't like cookies (and, or) ice cream.

5. I like music (and, or) art.

6. We will swim (and, or) play this weekend.

Writing

Read the paragraph. Circle each name that needs a capital letter. Write the names with capital letters in the list below.

(victor) called owen. victor asked owen to go to the park. owen walked his dog max to the park. ava was at the park, too.

Names

Victor _____

1. _____

2. _____

3. _____

4. _____

5. _____

6. _____

Name _____ Date _____

Vocabulary

A. **Fill in the missing letters to complete each word.**

1. wel _____   5. _____ joy

2. bui _____   6. _____ et

3. neighbor _____

4. wo _____

B. **Draw a line to match each word with the correct clue for it.**

8. work   a. People live here.

9. neighborhood   b. You put something together.

10. welcome   c. A job you do.

11. build   d. You get together with others.

12. project   e. This work takes a long time.

13. meet   f. You have fun.

14. enjoy   g. You say this to your friends.

Phonics

A. Circle the word that names the picture.

1.   star   stay

2.   cat   car

3.   soon   shark

4.   arm   aim

B. Circle the word with the *ar* sound.

5. more   mark   9. star   stop

6. farm   form   10. yak   yard

7. park   pork   11. small   smart

8. core   car   12. damp   dark

Name _____   Date _____

Think It Over

Reread to tell about the story.

My new friend is different from
me. In the country, he does not
live in a neighborhood with lots
of buildings. Country Mouse

lives on a big farm. There are many other animals
that live on the farm, like cows, pigs, and ducks.

**A. Circle the letter of the correct answer.
Then write the word.**

1. City Mouse has a new _____.

   a. sister   **c.** friend

   b. shirt   **d.** cousin

2. Country Mouse lives _____.

   a. in a neighborhood   **c.** in a park

   b. on a farm   **d.** in a sandbox

3. _____ live on the farm, too.

   a. tigers   **c.** lizards

   b. lions   **d.** pigs

B. Fill in the diagram to compare and contrast the city and the country. Put things that are the same in the middle. Put things that are different on one side or the other.

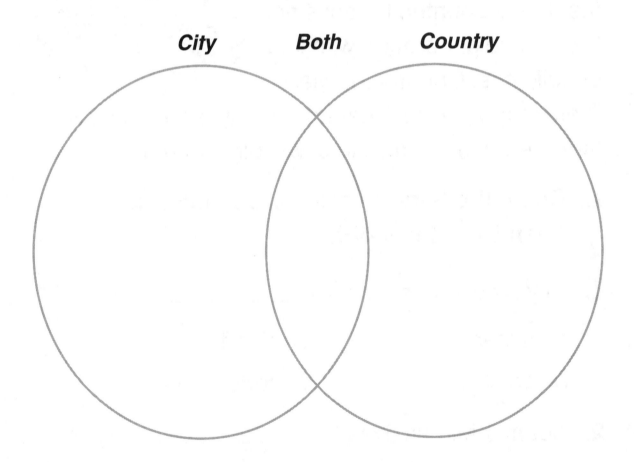

City   Both   Country

Name _____ Date _____

Grammar

Prepositions can tell us where something is.

Choose a preposition from the box. Write the preposition to complete each sentence.

in   inside   on   over   through   under

Example: Birds fly <u>in</u> the air.

1. Put the flour _____ the bowl.

2. Some bugs hide _____ rocks.

3. The horse jumped _____ the fence.

4. It is warm _____ the house.

5. Lizards run _____ the grass.

6. The book is _____ the table.

Writing

Choose the correct word. Write the sentence with the correct word.

Example: Do you (like, likes) hawks or lizards?
Do you like hawks or lizards?

1. Lizards (sit, sits) on rocks.

_____

- -

_____

2. They (run, runs) on the ground.

_____

- -

_____

3. A hawk (fly, flies) in the air.

_____

- -

_____

4. It (look, looks) for mice.

_____

- -

_____

Name _____ Date _____

Review

Answer the questions after reading Unit 6. You can go back and reread to help find the answers.

1. Circle all the words with an *oo* sound.

> Hear the cool tunes of Max and Ray. Max and Ray have fun at school.

2. What instrument does Max play?

_____

_____

3. What does Ray do? Circle the letter of the right answer.

   a. He plays the sax.
   b. He claps and sings.
   c. He swims in the pool.
   d. He swings in the park.

4. In *Owen and Mzee*, why does Owen need a dad?

_____

_____

_____

_____

5. Circle all the words with the *ar* sound.

> We worked hard and we worked together.
> Every town needs a nice park.

6. What are some things that Country Mouse and City Mouse do together?

7. Why are friends so important? Fill in the chart.

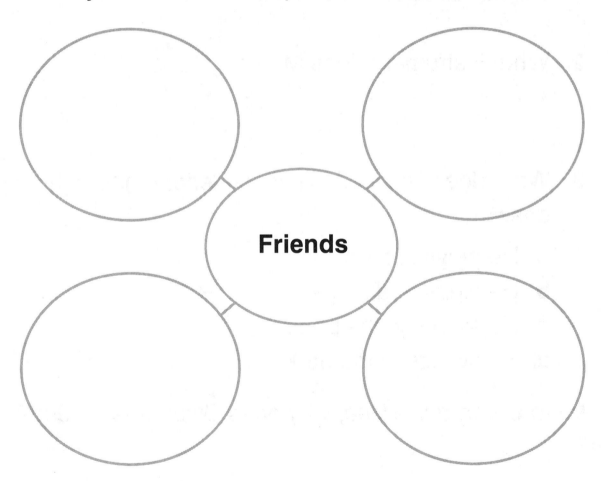

Friends

Name _____ Date _____

Writing Workshop: Write to Compare and Contrast

You will write a paragraph to compare and contrast. Read Kate's paragraph.

My two favorite sports are baseball and basketball. They are the same in some ways. You need a team and a ball for both. They are different, too. You need a bat for baseball. You need a hoop for basketball.

1. Prewrite Compare and contrast two sports or games. Write your ideas in the Venn diagram. How are they alike and different?

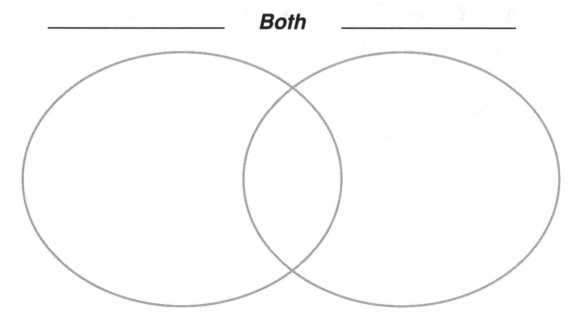

_____ **Both** _____

153

2. **Draft** Write a paragraph on the lines. Use the ideas from your Venn diagram.

_____

_____

_____

_____

_____

_____

_____

_____

_____

3 & 4. Revise and Edit Look for errors in your paragraph. Correct the errors to make your writing better. Go to page 169 of the Student Book and use the Editing Checklist.

5. **Publish** Make a clean copy of your paragraph on a sheet of paper. Share it with the class.

Name _____ Date _____

Fluency

A. Take turns reading the sentences with a partner. Use your finger to follow the words.

I left my book at school.

Dad's car is at the farm.

My mother is a nurse.

B. Read the sentences in Part A again. Draw a line from each sentence to the correct picture.

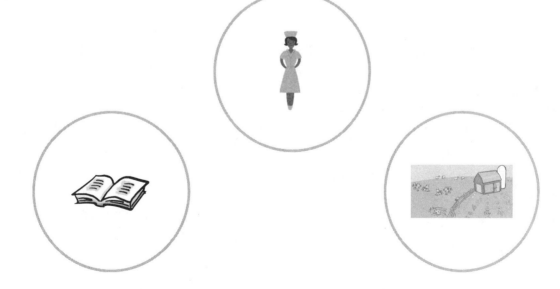

C. Take turns reading the sentences with a partner. Use your finger to follow the words. Read aloud for one minute. Count your words.

City Mouse and Country Mouse tells	6
about two mice who work together	12
to build a park for all the mice in the	22
neighborhood. City Mouse and Country	27
Mouse become friends. City Mouse learns	33
about farms and country life.	38

D. Read aloud to your teacher, friends, or family.

Name _____ Date _____

Learning Checklist

Phonics

☐ Letters: *oo*
☐ R-Controlled Vowels: *ir, er, ur*
☐ R-Controlled Vowels: *ar*

Strategies

☐ Find Main Idea and Details
☐ Summarize
☐ Prior Knowledge

Grammar

☐ Imperatives
☐ And/Or
☐ Prepositions

Writing

☐ Tell how to make something. Draw a picture of the steps.
☐ Draw a picture of Owen and Mzee. Compare them.
☐ Draw a picture of two animals. Compare and contrast them.
☐ Writing Workshop: Write to Compare and Contrast

Listening and Speaking

☐ An Interview